This Book Belong To:

_____

_____

_____

Calendar for Year 2022 (United States)

January

S	M	T	W	T	F	S
						1
2	3	4	5	6	7	8
9	10	11	12	13	14	15
16	17	18	19	20	21	22
23	24	25	26	27	28	29
30	31					

●:2 ◐:9 ○:17 ◑:25

February

S	M	T	W	T	F	S
		1	2	3	4	5
6	7	8	9	10	11	12
13	14	15	16	17	18	19
20	21	22	23	24	25	26
27	28					

●:1 ◐:8 ○:16 ◑:23

March

S	M	T	W	T	F	S
		1	2	3	4	5
6	7	8	9	10	11	12
13	14	15	16	17	18	19
20	21	22	23	24	25	26
27	28	29	30	31		

●:2 ◐:10 ○:18 ◑:25

April

S	M	T	W	T	F	S
					1	2
3	4	5	6	7	8	9
10	11	12	13	14	15	16
17	18	19	20	21	22	23
24	25	26	27	28	29	30

●:1 ◐:9 ○:16 ◑:23 ●:30

May

S	M	T	W	T	F	S
1	2	3	4	5	6	7
8	9	10	11	12	13	14
15	16	17	18	19	20	21
22	23	24	25	26	27	28
29	30	31				

◐:8 ○:16 ◑:22 ●:30

June

S	M	T	W	T	F	S
			1	2	3	4
5	6	7	8	9	10	11
12	13	14	15	16	17	18
19	20	21	22	23	24	25
26	27	28	29	30		

◐:7 ○:14 ◑:20 ●:28

July

S	M	T	W	T	F	S
					1	2
3	4	5	6	7	8	9
10	11	12	13	14	15	16
17	18	19	20	21	22	23
24	25	26	27	28	29	30
31						

◐:6 ○:13 ◑:20 ●:28

August

S	M	T	W	T	F	S
	1	2	3	4	5	6
7	8	9	10	11	12	13
14	15	16	17	18	19	20
21	22	23	24	25	26	27
28	29	30	31			

◐:5 ○:11 ◑:19 ●:27

September

S	M	T	W	T	F	S
				1	2	3
4	5	6	7	8	9	10
11	12	13	14	15	16	17
18	19	20	21	22	23	24
25	26	27	28	29	30	

◐:3 ○:10 ◑:17 ●:25

October

S	M	T	W	T	F	S
						1
2	3	4	5	6	7	8
9	10	11	12	13	14	15
16	17	18	19	20	21	22
23	24	25	26	27	28	29
30	31					

◐:2 ○:9 ◑:17 ●:25

November

S	M	T	W	T	F	S
		1	2	3	4	5
6	7	8	9	10	11	12
13	14	15	16	17	18	19
20	21	22	23	24	25	26
27	28	29	30			

◐:1 ○:8 ◑:16 ●:23 ◐:30

December

S	M	T	W	T	F	S
				1	2	3
4	5	6	7	8	9	10
11	12	13	14	15	16	17
18	19	20	21	22	23	24
25	26	27	28	29	30	31

○:7 ◑:16 ●:23 ◐:29

Jan 1	New Year's Day	Jul 4	Independence Day
Jan 17	Martin Luther King Jr. Day	Sep 5	Labor Day
Feb 14	Valentine's Day	Oct 10	Columbus Day (Most regions)
Feb 21	Presidents' Day (Most regions)	Oct 31	Halloween
Mar 17	St. Patrick's Day	Nov 11	Veterans Day
Apr 17	Easter Sunday	Nov 24	Thanksgiving Day
Apr 18	Tax Day	Nov 25	Black Friday
May 5	Cinco de Mayo	Dec 24	Christmas Eve
May 8	Mother's Day	Dec 25	Christmas Day
May 30	Memorial Day	Dec 26	'Christmas Day' observed
Jun 19	Father's Day	Dec 31	New Year's Eve

January 2022

Sunday	Monday	Tuesday	Wednesday
2	3	4	5
9	10	11	12
16	17	18	19
23 / 30	Martin Luther King 24 / 31	25	26

Hardships often prepare ordinary people
for an extraordinary destiny.
– C.S. Lewis

Thursday	Friday	Saturday	NOTES
		1 *New Year's Day*	
6	7	8	
13	14	15	
20	21	22	
27	28	29	

February 2022

Sunday	Monday	Tuesday	Wednesday
		1	2
6	7	8	9
13	14	15	16
20	21 *Presidents' Day*	22	23
27	28		

It's not whether you get knocked down.
It's whether you get up.
— Vince Lombardi

Thursday	Friday	Saturday	NOTES
3	4	5	
10	11	12	
17	18	19	
24	25	26	

March 2022

Sunday	Monday	Tuesday	Wednesday
		1	2
6	7	8	9
13	14	15	16
20	21	22	23
27	28	29	30

Whatever you hold in your mind on a consistent basis
is exactly what you will experience in your life.
— Tony Robbins

Thursday	Friday	Saturday	NOTES
3	4	5	
10	11	12	
17	18	19	
St. Patrick's Day			
24	25	26	
31			

April 2022

Sunday	Monday	Tuesday	Wednesday
3	4	5	6
10	11	12	13
17	18	19	20
Easter Sunday	*Tax Day*		
24	25	26	27

Perseverance is the hard work you do after you get tired
of doing the hard work you already did.
— Newt Gingrich

Thursday	Friday	Saturday	NOTES
	1	2	
7	8	9	
14	15	16	
21	22	23	
28	29	30	

May 2022

Sunday	Monday	Tuesday	Wednesday
1	2	3	4
8 *Mother's Day*	9	10	11
15	16	17	18
22	23	24	25
29	30 *Memorial Day*	31	

Don't wish it were easier.
Wish you were better. — Jim Rohn

Thursday	Friday	Saturday	NOTES
5 *Cinco de Mayo*	6	7	
12	13	14	
19	20	21	
26	27	28	

June 2022

Sunday	Monday	Tuesday	Wednesday
			1
5	6	7	8
12	13	14	15
19 *Father's Day*	20	21	22
26	27	28	29

Perfection is not attainable,
but if we chase perfection we can catch excellence.
— *Vince Lombardi*

Thursday	Friday	Saturday	NOTES
2	3	4	
9	10	11	
16	17	18	
23	24	25	
30			

July 2022

Sunday	Monday	Tuesday	Wednesday
3	4	5	6
	Independence Day		
10	11	12	13
17	18	19	20
24	25	26	27
31			

Only those who dare to fail greatly
can ever achieve greatly. — Robert F. Kennedy

Thursday	Friday	Saturday	NOTES
	1	2	
7	8	9	
14	15	16	
21	22	23	
28	29	30	

August 2022

Sunday	Monday	Tuesday	Wednesday
	1	2	3
7	8	9	10
14	15	16	17
21	22	23	24
28	29	30	31

Thursday	Friday	Saturday	NOTES
4	5	6	
11	12	13	
18	19	20	
25	26	27	

September 2022

Sunday	Monday	Tuesday	Wednesday
4	5 *Labor Day*	6	7
11	12	13	14
18	19	20	21
25	26	27	28

You will never find time for anything.
If you want time you must make it. — Charles Buxton

Thursday	Friday	Saturday	NOTES
1	2	3	
8	9	10	
15	16	17	
22	23	24	
29	30		

October 2022

Sunday	Monday	Tuesday	Wednesday
2	3	4	5
9	10 _Columbus Day_	11	12
16	17	18	19
23 / 30	24 / 31 _Halloween_	25	26

Thursday	Friday	Saturday	NOTES
		1	
6	7	8	
13	14	15	
20	21	22	
27	28	29	

November 2022

Sunday	Monday	Tuesday	Wednesday
		1	2
6	7	8	9
13	14	15	16
20	21	22	23
27	28	29	30

I have not failed.
I've just found 10,000 ways that won't work.
~Thomas A. Edison

Thursday	Friday	Saturday	NOTES
3	4	5	
10	11 *Veterans Day*	12	
17	18	19	
24 *Thanksgiving Day*	25	26	

December 2022

Sunday	Monday	Tuesday	Wednesday
4	5	6	7
11	12	13	14
18	19	20	21
25	26	27	28

Christmas Day

When you stop chasing the wrong things
you give the right things a chance to catch you.
~Lolly Daskal

Thursday	Friday	Saturday	NOTES
1	2	3	
8	9	10	
15	16	17	
22	23	24	
29	30	31	

Calendar for Year 2023 (United States)

January

S	M	T	W	T	F	S
1	2	3	4	5	6	7
8	9	10	11	12	13	14
15	16	17	18	19	20	21
22	23	24	25	26	27	28
29	30	31				

○: 6 ◐: 14 ●: 21 ◑: 28

February

S	M	T	W	T	F	S
			1	2	3	4
5	6	7	8	9	10	11
12	13	14	15	16	17	18
19	20	21	22	23	24	25
26	27	28				

○: 5 ◐: 13 ●: 20 ◑: 27

March

S	M	T	W	T	F	S
			1	2	3	4
5	6	7	8	9	10	11
12	13	14	15	16	17	18
19	20	21	22	23	24	25
26	27	28	29	30	31	

○: 7 ◐: 14 ●: 21 ◑: 28

April

S	M	T	W	T	F	S
						1
2	3	4	5	6	7	8
9	10	11	12	13	14	15
16	17	18	19	20	21	22
23	24	25	26	27	28	29
30						

○: 6 ◐: 13 ●: 20 ◑: 27

May

S	M	T	W	T	F	S
	1	2	3	4	5	6
7	8	9	10	11	12	13
14	15	16	17	18	19	20
21	22	23	24	25	26	27
28	29	30	31			

○: 5 ◐: 12 ●: 19 ◑: 27

June

S	M	T	W	T	F	S
				1	2	3
4	5	6	7	8	9	10
11	12	13	14	15	16	17
18	19	20	21	22	23	24
25	26	27	28	29	30	

○: 3 ◐: 10 ●: 18 ◑: 26

July

S	M	T	W	T	F	S
						1
2	3	4	5	6	7	8
9	10	11	12	13	14	15
16	17	18	19	20	21	22
23	24	25	26	27	28	29
30	31					

○: 3 ◐: 9 ●: 17 ◑: 25

August

S	M	T	W	T	F	S
		1	2	3	4	5
6	7	8	9	10	11	12
13	14	15	16	17	18	19
20	21	22	23	24	25	26
27	28	29	30	31		

○: 1 ◐: 8 ●: 16 ◑: 24 ○: 30

September

S	M	T	W	T	F	S
					1	2
3	4	5	6	7	8	9
10	11	12	13	14	15	16
17	18	19	20	21	22	23
24	25	26	27	28	29	30

◐: 6 ●: 14 ◑: 22 ○: 29

October

S	M	T	W	T	F	S
1	2	3	4	5	6	7
8	9	10	11	12	13	14
15	16	17	18	19	20	21
22	23	24	25	26	27	28
29	30	31				

◐: 6 ●: 14 ◑: 21 ○: 28

November

S	M	T	W	T	F	S
			1	2	3	4
5	6	7	8	9	10	11
12	13	14	15	16	17	18
19	20	21	22	23	24	25
26	27	28	29	30		

◐: 5 ●: 13 ◑: 20 ○: 27

December

S	M	T	W	T	F	S
					1	2
3	4	5	6	7	8	9
10	11	12	13	14	15	16
17	18	19	20	21	22	23
24	25	26	27	28	29	30
31						

◐: 5 ●: 12 ◑: 19 ○: 26

Jan 1	New Year's Day		Jun 18	Father's Day
Jan 2	'New Year's Day' observed		Jul 4	Independence Day
Jan 16	Martin Luther King Jr. Day		Sep 4	Labor Day
Feb 14	Valentine's Day		Oct 9	Columbus Day (Most regions)
Feb 20	Presidents' Day (Most regions)		Oct 31	Halloween
Mar 17	St. Patrick's Day		Nov 10	Veterans Day observed
Apr 9	Easter Sunday		Nov 11	Veterans Day
Apr 17	Tax Day		Nov 23	Thanksgiving Day
May 5	Cinco de Mayo		Nov 24	Black Friday
May 14	Mother's Day		Dec 24	Christmas Eve
May 29	Memorial Day		Dec 25	Christmas Day

January 2023

Sunday	Monday	Tuesday	Wednesday
1 *New Year's Day*	2 *New Year's Day (observed)*	3	4
8	9	10	11
15	16 *Martin Luther King*	17	18
22	23	24	25
29	30	31	

Success is not final, failure is not fatal:
it is the courage to continue that counts.
– Winston Churchill

Thursday	Friday	Saturday	NOTES
5	6	7	
12	13	14	
19	20	21	
26	27	28	

February 2023

Sunday	Monday	Tuesday	Wednesday
			1
5	6	7	8
12	13	14	15
19	20 *Presidents' Day*	21	22
26	27	28	

There is only one thing that makes a dream impossible to achieve: the fear of failure.
— Paulo Coelho

Thursday	Friday	Saturday	NOTES
2	3	4	
9	10	11	
16	17	18	
23	24	25	

March 2023

Sunday	Monday	Tuesday	Wednesday
			1
5	6	7	8
12	13	14	15
19	20	21	22
26	27	28	29

Start by doing what's necessary; then do what's possible;
and suddenly you are doing the impossible.
— Francis of Assisi

Thursday	Friday	Saturday	NOTES
2	3	4	
9	10	11	
16	17	18	
	St. Patrick's Day		
23	24	25	
30	31		

April 2023

Sunday	Monday	Tuesday	Wednesday
2	3	4	5
9 *Easter Sunday*	10	11	12
16	17 *Tax Day*	18	19
23 30	24	25	26

Strength does not come from physical capacity.
It comes from an indomitable will.
– Mahatma Gandhi

Thursday	Friday	Saturday	NOTES
		1	
6	7	8	
13	14	15	
20	21	22	
27	28	29	

May 2023

Sunday	Monday	Tuesday	Wednesday
	1	2	3
7	8	9	10
14 *Mother's Day*	15	16	17
21	22	23	24
28	29 *Memorial Day*	30	31

Whatever the mind can conceive and believe,
it can achieve. — Napoleon Hill

Thursday	Friday	Saturday	NOTES
4	5	6	
	Cinco de Mayo		
11	12	13	
18	19	20	
25	26	27	

June 2023

Sunday	Monday	Tuesday	Wednesday
4	5	6	7
11	12	13	14
18	19	20	21
Father's Day			
25	26	27	28

The only person you are destined to become
is the person you decide to be. —Ralph Waldo Emerson

Thursday	Friday	Saturday	NOTES
1	2	3	
8	9	10	
15	16	17	
22	23	24	
29	30		

July 2023

Sunday	Monday	Tuesday	Wednesday
2	3	4 *Independence Day*	5
9	10	11	12
16	17	18	19
23 / 30	24 / 31	25	26

*Setting goals is the first step
into turning the invisible into the visible. — Tony Robbins*

Thursday	Friday	Saturday	NOTES
		1	
6	7	8	
13	14	15	
20	21	22	
27	28	29	

August 2023

Sunday	Monday	Tuesday	Wednesday
		1	2
6	7	8	9
13	14	15	16
20	21	22	23
27	28	29	30

Your time is limited,
so don't waste it living someone else's life. — Steve Jobs

Thursday	Friday	Saturday	NOTES
3	4	5	
10	11	12	
17	18	19	
24	25	26	
31			

September 2023

Sunday	Monday	Tuesday	Wednesday
3	4	5	6
	Labor Day		
10	11	12	13
17	18	19	20
24	25	26	27

The pessimist sees difficulty in every opportunity.
The optimist sees opportunity in every difficulty.
— Winston Churchill

Thursday	Friday	Saturday	NOTES
	1	2	
7	8	9	
14	15	16	
21	22	23	
28	29	30	

October 2023

Sunday	Monday	Tuesday	Wednesday
1	2	3	4
8	9 *Columbus Day*	10	11
15	16	17	18
22	23	24	25
29	30	31 *Halloween*	

Thursday	Friday	Saturday	NOTES
5	6	7	
12	13	14	
19	20	21	
26	27	28	

November 2023

Sunday	Monday	Tuesday	Wednesday
			1
5	6	7	8
12	13	14	15
19	20	21	22
26	27	28	29

Great minds discuss ideas; average minds discuss events;
small minds discuss people. ~Eleanor Roosevelt

Thursday	Friday	Saturday	NOTES
2	3	4	
9	10	11 *Veterans Day*	
16	17	18	
23 *Thanksgiving Day*	24	25	
30			

December 2023

Sunday	Monday	Tuesday	Wednesday
3	4	5	6
10	11	12	13
17	18	19	20
24	25	26	27
31 *Christmas Day*			

*The distance between insanity and genius
is measured only by success. ~Bruce Feirstein*

Thursday	Friday	Saturday
	1	2
7	8	9
14	15	16
21	22	23
28	29	30

NOTES

Calendar for Year 2024

January

S	M	T	W	T	F	S
	1	2	3	4	5	6
7	8	9	10	11	12	13
14	15	16	17	18	19	20
21	22	23	24	25	26	27
28	29	30	31			

◑:3　●:11　◐:17　○:25

February

S	M	T	W	T	F	S
				1	2	3
4	5	6	7	8	9	10
11	12	13	14	15	16	17
18	19	20	21	22	23	24
25	26	27	28	29		

◑:2　●:9　◐:16　○:24

March

S	M	T	W	T	F	S
					1	2
3	4	5	6	7	8	9
10	11	12	13	14	15	16
17	18	19	20	21	22	23
24	25	26	27	28	29	30
31						

◑:3　●:10　◐:17　○:25

April

S	M	T	W	T	F	S
	1	2	3	4	5	6
7	8	9	10	11	12	13
14	15	16	17	18	19	20
21	22	23	24	25	26	27
28	29	30				

◑:1　●:8　◐:15　○:23

May

S	M	T	W	T	F	S
			1	2	3	4
5	6	7	8	9	10	11
12	13	14	15	16	17	18
19	20	21	22	23	24	25
26	27	28	29	30	31	

◑:1　●:7　◐:15　○:23　◑:30

June

S	M	T	W	T	F	S
						1
2	3	4	5	6	7	8
9	10	11	12	13	14	15
16	17	18	19	20	21	22
23	24	25	26	27	28	29
30						

●:6　◐:14　○:21　◑:28

July

S	M	T	W	T	F	S
	1	2	3	4	5	6
7	8	9	10	11	12	13
14	15	16	17	18	19	20
21	22	23	24	25	26	27
28	29	30	31			

●:5　◐:13　○:21　◑:27

August

S	M	T	W	T	F	S
				1	2	3
4	5	6	7	8	9	10
11	12	13	14	15	16	17
18	19	20	21	22	23	24
25	26	27	28	29	30	31

●:4　◐:12　○:19　◑:26

September

S	M	T	W	T	F	S
1	2	3	4	5	6	7
8	9	10	11	12	13	14
15	16	17	18	19	20	21
22	23	24	25	26	27	28
29	30					

●:2　◐:11　○:17　◑:24

October

S	M	T	W	T	F	S
		1	2	3	4	5
6	7	8	9	10	11	12
13	14	15	16	17	18	19
20	21	22	23	24	25	26
27	28	29	30	31		

●:2　◐:10　○:17　◑:24

November

S	M	T	W	T	F	S
					1	2
3	4	5	6	7	8	9
10	11	12	13	14	15	16
17	18	19	20	21	22	23
24	25	26	27	28	29	30

●:1　◐:9　○:15　◑:22

December

S	M	T	W	T	F	S
1	2	3	4	5	6	7
8	9	10	11	12	13	14
15	16	17	18	19	20	21
22	23	24	25	26	27	28
29	30	31				

●:1　◐:8　○:15　◑:22　●:30

Jan 1 ● New Year's Day	**May 5** ● Cinco de Mayo	**Nov 5** ● Election Day
Jan 15 ● Martin Luther King Jr. Day	**May 12** ● Mother's Day	**Nov 11** ● Veterans Day
Feb 14 ● Valentine's Day	**May 27** ● Memorial Day	**Nov 28** ● Thanksgiving Day
Feb 19 ● Presidents' Day (Most regions)	**Jun 16** ● Father's Day	**Nov 29** ● Black Friday
Mar 17 ● St. Patrick's Day	**Jul 4** ● Independence Day	**Dec 24** ● Christmas Eve
Mar 31 ● Easter Sunday	**Sep 2** ● Labor Day	**Dec 25** ● Christmas Day
Apr 1 ● Easter Monday	**Oct 14** ● Columbus Day (Most regions)	**Dec 31** ● New Year's Eve
Apr 15 ● Tax Day	**Oct 31** ● Halloween	

January 2024

Sunday	Monday	Tuesday	Wednesday
	1 *New Year's Day*	2	3
7	8	9	10
14	15 *Martin Luther King*	16	17
21	22	23	24
28	29	30	31

"Successful people do what unsuccessful people are not willing to do.
Don't wish it were easier; wish you were better."
-- Jim Rohn

Thursday	Friday	Saturday	NOTES
4	5	6	
11	12	13	
18	19	20	
25	26	27	

February 2024

Sunday	Monday	Tuesday	Wednesday
4	5	6	7
11	12	13	14
18	19 *Presidents' Day*	20	21
25	26	27	28

"I owe my success to having listened respectfully to the very best advice, and then going away and doing the exact opposite."
-- *G. K. Chesterton*

Thursday	Friday	Saturday	NOTES
1	2	3	
8	9	10	
15	16	17	
22	23	24	
29			

March 2024

Sunday	Monday	Tuesday	Wednesday
3	4	5	6
10	11	12	13
17 *St. Patrick's Day*	18	19	20
24 / 31 *Easter Sunday*	25	26	27

"The ones who are crazy enough to think they can change the world, are the ones that do."
-- Anonymous

Thursday	Friday	Saturday	NOTES
	1	2	
7	8	9	
14	15	16	
21	22	23	
28	29	30	

April 2024

Sunday	Monday	Tuesday	Wednesday
	1	2	3
	Easter Monday		
7	8	9	10
14	15	16	17
	Tax Day		
21	22	23	24
28	29	30	

"There are no secrets to success. It is the result of preparation, hard work, and learning from failure."
-- Colin Powell

Thursday	Friday	Saturday	NOTES
4	5	6	
11	12	13	
18	19	20	
25	26	27	

May 2024

Sunday	Monday	Tuesday	Wednesday
			1
5	6	7	8
Cinco de Mayo			
12	13	14	15
Mother's Day			
19	20	21	22
26	27	28	29
	Memorial Day		

"If you can dream it, you can do it."

-- Walt Disney

Thursday	Friday	Saturday	NOTES
2	3	4	
9	10	11	
16	17	18	
23	24	25	
30	31		

June 2024

Sunday	Monday	Tuesday	Wednesday
2	3	4	5
9	10	11	12
16	17	18	19
Father's Day 23 / 30	24	25	26

"Many of life's failures are people who did not realize how close they were to success when they gave up."
— *Thomas Edison*

Thursday	Friday	Saturday	NOTES
		1	
6	7	8	
13	14	15	
20	21	22	
27	28	29	

July 2024

Sunday	Monday	Tuesday	Wednesday
	1	2	3
7	8	9	10
14	15	16	17
21	22	23	24
28	29	30	31

"I never dreamed about success,
I worked for it."
-- Estee Lauder

Thursday	Friday	Saturday	NOTES
4	5	6	
Independence Day			
11	12	13	
18	19	20	
25	26	27	

August 2024

Sunday	Monday	Tuesday	Wednesday
4	5	6	7
11	12	13	14
18	19	20	21
25	26	27	28

"There is a powerful driving force inside every human being that, once unleashed, can make any vision, dream, or desire a reality."
-- Anthony Robbins

Thursday	Friday	Saturday	NOTES
1	2	3	
8	9	10	
15	16	17	
22	23	24	
29	30	31	

September 2024

Sunday	Monday	Tuesday	Wednesday
1	2 *Labor Day*	3	4
8	9	10	11
15	16	17	18
22	23	24	25
29	30		

"Leadership is more than just being able to cross the t's and dot the i's.
It's about character and integrity and work ethic."
- Steve Largent

Thursday	Friday	Saturday	NOTES
5	6	7	
12	13	14	
19	20	21	
26	27	28	

October 2024

Sunday	Monday	Tuesday	Wednesday
		1	2
6	7	8	9
13	14	15	16
	Columbus Day		
20	21	22	23
27	28	29	30

"The best way to learn is by doing. The only way to build a strong work ethic is getting your hands dirty."
- Alex Spanos

Thursday	Friday	Saturday	NOTES
3	4	5	
10	11	12	
17	18	19	
24	25	26	
31			

Halloween

November 2024

Sunday	Monday	Tuesday	Wednesday
3	4	5	6
10	11 *Veterans Day*	12	13
17	18	19	20
24	25	26	27

"Enjoy life, study hard, play hard, be kind to other people,
set high standards, and don't be afraid to say "No."'
— *Nia Long*

Thursday	Friday	Saturday	NOTES
	1	2	
7	8	9	
14	15	16	
21	22	23	
28	29	30	

Thanksgiving Day

December 2024

Sunday	Monday	Tuesday	Wednesday
1	2	3	4
8	9	10	11
15	16	17	18
22	23	24	25 *Christmas Day*
29	30	31	

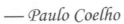
"When we strive to become better than we are,
everything around us becomes better too."
— *Paulo Coelho*

Thursday	Friday	Saturday	NOTES
5	6	7	
12	13	14	
19	20	21	
26	27	28	

Calendar for Year 2025 (United States)

January

S	M	T	W	T	F	S
			1	2	3	4
5	6	7	8	9	10	11
12	13	14	15	16	17	18
19	20	21	22	23	24	25
26	27	28	29	30	31	

◐:6   ○:13   ◑:21   ●:29

February

S	M	T	W	T	F	S
						1
2	3	4	5	6	7	8
9	10	11	12	13	14	15
16	17	18	19	20	21	22
23	24	25	26	27	28	

◐:5   ○:12   ◑:20   ●:27

March

S	M	T	W	T	F	S
						1
2	3	4	5	6	7	8
9	10	11	12	13	14	15
16	17	18	19	20	21	22
23	24	25	26	27	28	29
30	31					

◐:6   ○:14   ◑:22   ●:29

April

S	M	T	W	T	F	S
		1	2	3	4	5
6	7	8	9	10	11	12
13	14	15	16	17	18	19
20	21	22	23	24	25	26
27	28	29	30			

◐:4   ○:12   ◑:20   ●:27

May

S	M	T	W	T	F	S
				1	2	3
4	5	6	7	8	9	10
11	12	13	14	15	16	17
18	19	20	21	22	23	24
25	26	27	28	29	30	31

◐:4   ○:12   ◑:20   ●:26

June

S	M	T	W	T	F	S
1	2	3	4	5	6	7
8	9	10	11	12	13	14
15	16	17	18	19	20	21
22	23	24	25	26	27	28
29	30					

◐:2   ○:11   ◑:18   ●:25

July

S	M	T	W	T	F	S
		1	2	3	4	5
6	7	8	9	10	11	12
13	14	15	16	17	18	19
20	21	22	23	24	25	26
27	28	29	30	31		

◐:2   ○:10   ◑:17   ●:24

August

S	M	T	W	T	F	S
					1	2
3	4	5	6	7	8	9
10	11	12	13	14	15	16
17	18	19	20	21	22	23
24	25	26	27	28	29	30
31						

◐:1   ○:9   ◑:16   ●:23   ◐:31

September

S	M	T	W	T	F	S
	1	2	3	4	5	6
7	8	9	10	11	12	13
14	15	16	17	18	19	20
21	22	23	24	25	26	27
28	29	30				

○:7   ◑:14   ●:21   ◐:29

October

S	M	T	W	T	F	S
			1	2	3	4
5	6	7	8	9	10	11
12	13	14	15	16	17	18
19	20	21	22	23	24	25
26	27	28	29	30	31	

○:6   ◑:13   ●:21   ◐:29

November

S	M	T	W	T	F	S
						1
2	3	4	5	6	7	8
9	10	11	12	13	14	15
16	17	18	19	20	21	22
23	24	25	26	27	28	29
30						

○:5   ◑:12   ●:20   ◐:28

December

S	M	T	W	T	F	S
	1	2	3	4	5	6
7	8	9	10	11	12	13
14	15	16	17	18	19	20
21	22	23	24	25	26	27
28	29	30	31			

○:4   ◑:11   ●:19   ◐:27

Jan 1 ● New Year's Day		**May 5** ● Cinco de Mayo		**Nov 11** ● Veterans Day	
Jan 20 ● Martin Luther King Jr. Day		**May 11** ● Mother's Day		**Nov 27** ● Thanksgiving Day	
Feb 14 ● Valentine's Day		**May 26** ● Memorial Day		**Nov 28** ● Black Friday	
Feb 17 ● Presidents' Day (Most regions)		**Jun 15** ● Father's Day		**Dec 24** ● Christmas Eve	
Mar 17 ● St. Patrick's Day		**Jul 4** ● Independence Day		**Dec 25** ● Christmas Day	
Apr 15 ● Tax Day		**Sep 1** ● Labor Day		**Dec 31** ● New Year's Eve	
Apr 20 ● Easter Sunday		**Oct 13** ● Columbus Day (Most regions)			
Apr 21 ● Easter Monday		**Oct 31** ● Halloween			

January 2025

Sunday	Monday	Tuesday	Wednesday
			1 *New Year's Day*
5	6	7	8
12	13	14	15
19	20 *Martin Luther King*	21	22
26	27	28	29

Thursday	Friday	Saturday	NOTES
2	3	4	_____
9	10	11	_____
16	17	18	_____
23	24	25	_____
30	31		_____

February 2025

Sunday	Monday	Tuesday	Wednesday
2	3	4	5
9	10	11	12
16	17	18	19
	Presidents' Day		
23	24	25	26

Thursday	Friday	Saturday	NOTES
		1	
6	7	8	
13	14	15	
	Valentine's Day		
20	21	22	
27	28		

March 2025

Sunday	Monday	Tuesday	Wednesday
2	3	4	5
9	10	11	12
16	17	18	19
23	24 *St. Patrick's Day*	25	26
30	31		

"If you think you are too small to make a difference,
try sleeping with a mosquito."
-- Dalai Lama

Thursday	Friday	Saturday	NOTES
		1	
6	7	8	
13	14	15	
20	21	22	
27	28	29	

April 2025

Sunday	Monday	Tuesday	Wednesday
		1	2
6	7	8	9
13	14	15 *Tax Day*	16
20 *Easter Sunday*	21 *Easter Monday*	22	23
27	28	29	30

"Have no fear of perfection. You'll never reach it."
-- *Salvador Dali*

Thursday	Friday	Saturday	NOTES
3	4	5	
10	11	12	
17	18	19	
24	25	26	

May 2025

Sunday	Monday	Tuesday	Wednesday
4	5 *Cinco de Mayo*	6	7
11 *Mother's Day*	12	13	14
18	19	20	21
25	26 *Memorial Day*	27	28

"You can change. And you can be an agent of change."
-- Laura Dern

Thursday	Friday	Saturday	NOTES
1	2	3	
8	9	10	
15	16	17	
22	23	24	
29	30	31	

June 2025

Sunday	Monday	Tuesday	Wednesday
1	2	3	4
8	9	10	11
15 *Father's Day*	16	17	18
22	23	24	25
29	30		

"Hard work and education will take you farther than any government program can ever promise."
-- Mia Love

Thursday	Friday	Saturday	NOTES
5	6	7	
12	13	14	
19	20	21	
26	27	28	

July 2025

Sunday	Monday	Tuesday	Wednesday
		1	2
6	7	8	9
13	14	15	16
20	21	22	23
27	28	29	30

"Wanting to be a good actor is not good enough.
You must want to be a great actor. You just have to have that."
-- Gary Oldman

Thursday	Friday	Saturday	NOTES
3	4	5	
	Independence Day		
10	11	12	
17	18	19	
24	25	26	
31			

August 2025

Sunday	Monday	Tuesday	Wednesday
3	4	5	6
10	11	12	13
17	18	19	20
24 / 31	25	26	27

"Life has a much bigger plan for you. Happiness is part of that plan. Health is part of that plan. Stability is part of that plan. Constant struggle is not."
-- Kris Carr

Thursday	Friday	Saturday	NOTES
	1	2	_____
			_____
			_____
			_____
7	8	9	_____
			_____
			_____
14	15	16	_____
			_____
			_____
21	22	23	_____
			_____
			_____
28	29	30	_____
			_____
			_____

September 2025

Sunday	Monday	Tuesday	Wednesday
	1 Labor Day	2	3
7	8	9	10
14	15	16	17
21	22	23	24
28	29	30	

"Just believe in yourself. Even if you don't,
pretend that you do and, at some point, you will."
-- Venus Williams

Thursday	Friday	Saturday	NOTES
4	5	6	
11	12	13	
18	19	20	
25	26	27	

October 2025

Sunday	Monday	Tuesday	Wednesday
			1
5	6	7	8
12	13 *Columbus Day*	14	15
19	20	21	22
26	27	28	29

"The first step is clearly defining what it is you're after, because without knowing that, you'll never get it."
-- Halle Berry

Thursday	Friday	Saturday	NOTES
2	3	4	
9	10	11	
16	17	18	
23	24	25	
30	31 *Halloween*		

November 2025

Sunday	Monday	Tuesday	Wednesday
2	3	4	5
9	10	11 *Veterans Day*	12
16	17	18	19
23 / 30	24	25	26

"What gets celebrated gets replicated."
-- Bradley Cooper

Thursday	Friday	Saturday	NOTES
		1	
6	7	8	
13	14	15	
20	21	22	
27 *Thanksgiving Day*	28 *Black Friday*	29	

December 2025

Sunday	Monday	Tuesday	Wednesday
	1	2	3
7	8	9	10
14	15	16	17
21	22	23	24
28	29	30	31

"Far and away the best prize that life has to offer is the chance to work hard at work worth doing."
-- Theodore Roosevelt

Thursday	Friday	Saturday
4	5	6
11	12	13
18	19	20
25 *Christmas Day*	26	27

NOTES

_____
_____
_____
_____
_____
_____
_____
_____
_____
_____
_____
_____
_____
_____
_____
_____
_____
_____
_____
_____
_____
_____
_____
_____

Calendar for Year 2026 (United States)

January

S	M	T	W	T	F	S
				1	2	3
4	5	6	7	8	9	10
11	12	13	14	15	16	17
18	19	20	21	22	23	24
25	26	27	28	29	30	31

○:3　◑:10　●:18　◐:25

February

S	M	T	W	T	F	S
1	2	3	4	5	6	7
8	9	10	11	12	13	14
15	16	17	18	19	20	21
22	23	24	25	26	27	28

○:1　◑:9　●:17　◐:24

March

S	M	T	W	T	F	S
1	2	3	4	5	6	7
8	9	10	11	12	13	14
15	16	17	18	19	20	21
22	23	24	25	26	27	28
29	30	31				

○:3　◑:11　●:18　◐:25

April

S	M	T	W	T	F	S
			1	2	3	4
5	6	7	8	9	10	11
12	13	14	15	16	17	18
19	20	21	22	23	24	25
26	27	28	29	30		

○:1　◑:10　●:17　◐:23

May

S	M	T	W	T	F	S
					1	2
3	4	5	6	7	8	9
10	11	12	13	14	15	16
17	18	19	20	21	22	23
24	25	26	27	28	29	30
31						

○:1　◑:9　●:16　◐:23　○:31

June

S	M	T	W	T	F	S
	1	2	3	4	5	6
7	8	9	10	11	12	13
14	15	16	17	18	19	20
21	22	23	24	25	26	27
28	29	30				

◑:8　●:14　◐:21　○:29

July

S	M	T	W	T	F	S
			1	2	3	4
5	6	7	8	9	10	11
12	13	14	15	16	17	18
19	20	21	22	23	24	25
26	27	28	29	30	31	

◑:7　●:14　◐:21　○:29

August

S	M	T	W	T	F	S
						1
2	3	4	5	6	7	8
9	10	11	12	13	14	15
16	17	18	19	20	21	22
23	24	25	26	27	28	29
30	31					

◑:5　●:12　◐:19　○:28

September

S	M	T	W	T	F	S
		1	2	3	4	5
6	7	8	9	10	11	12
13	14	15	16	17	18	19
20	21	22	23	24	25	26
27	28	29	30			

◑:4　●:10　◐:18　○:26

October

S	M	T	W	T	F	S
				1	2	3
4	5	6	7	8	9	10
11	12	13	14	15	16	17
18	19	20	21	22	23	24
25	26	27	28	29	30	31

◑:3　●:10　◐:18　○:26

November

S	M	T	W	T	F	S
1	2	3	4	5	6	7
8	9	10	11	12	13	14
15	16	17	18	19	20	21
22	23	24	25	26	27	28
29	30					

◑:1　●:9　◐:17　○:24

December

S	M	T	W	T	F	S
		1	2	3	4	5
6	7	8	9	10	11	12
13	14	15	16	17	18	19
20	21	22	23	24	25	26
27	28	29	30	31		

◑:1　●:8　◐:17　○:23　◑:30

Jan 1	● New Year's Day	May 5	● Cinco de Mayo	Oct 31	● Halloween
Jan 19	● Martin Luther King Jr. Day	May 10	● Mother's Day	Nov 11	● Veterans Day
Feb 14	● Valentine's Day	May 25	● Memorial Day	Nov 26	● Thanksgiving Day
Feb 16	● Presidents' Day (Most regions)	Jun 21	● Father's Day	Nov 27	● Black Friday
Mar 17	● St. Patrick's Day	Jul 3	● 'Independence Day' observed	Dec 24	● Christmas Eve
Apr 5	● Easter Sunday	Jul 4	● Independence Day	Dec 25	● Christmas Day
Apr 6	● Easter Monday	Sep 7	● Labor Day	Dec 31	● New Year's Eve
Apr 15	● Tax Day	Oct 12	● Columbus Day (Most regions)		

January 2026

Sunday	Monday	Tuesday	Wednesday
4	5	6	7
11	12	13	14
18	19 *Martin Luther King Jr. Day*	20	21
25	26	27	28

"You can't do it unless you can imagine it."
-- George Lucas

Thursday	Friday	Saturday	NOTES
1 *New Year's Day*	2	3	
8	9	10	
15	16	17	
22	23	24	
29	30	31	

February 2026

Sunday	Monday	Tuesday	Wednesday
1	2	3	4
8	9	10	11
15	16 President's Day	17	18
22	23	24	25

"Let me tell you the secret that has led me to my goal.
My strength lies solely in my tenacity."
-- Louis Pasteur

Thursday	Friday	Saturday	NOTES
5	6	7	
12	13	14 *Valentine's Day*	
19	20	21	
26	27	28	

March 2026

Sunday	Monday	Tuesday	Wednesday
1	2	3	4
8	9	10	11
15	16	17 *St. Patrick's Day*	18
22	23	24	25
29	30	31	

"Everyone has a plan 'till they get punched in the mouth."
-- Mike Tyson

Thursday	Friday	Saturday	NOTES
5	6	7	
12	13	14	
19	20	21	
26	27	28	

April 2026

Sunday	Monday	Tuesday	Wednesday
			1
5 *Easter Sunday*	6 *Easter Monday*	7	8
12	13	14	15 *Tax Day*
19	20	21	22
26	27	28	29

"Work hard and believe in yourself
even when nobody else believes in you."
-- Richard Sherman

Thursday	Friday	Saturday	NOTES
2	3	4	
9	10	11	
16	17	18	
23	24	25	
30			

May 2026

Sunday	Monday	Tuesday	Wednesday
3	4	5 *Cinco de Mayo*	6
10 *Mother's Day*	11	12	13
17	18	19	20
24	25	26	27
31 *Memorial Day*			

"I think happiness is overrated. Satisfied,
at peace-those would be more realistic goals."
-- Brad Pitt

Thursday	Friday	Saturday	NOTES
	1	2	
7	8	9	
14	15	16	
21	22	23	
28	29	30	

June 2026

Sunday	Monday	Tuesday	Wednesday
	1	2	3
7	8	9	10
14	15	16	17
21	22	23	24
Father's Day			
28	29	30	

"Normality is a paved road: It's comfortable to walk,
but no flowers grow on it."
-- Vincent Van Gogh

Thursday	Friday	Saturday	NOTES
4	5	6	
11	12	13	
18	19	20	
25	26	27	

July 2026

Sunday	Monday	Tuesday	Wednesday
			1
5	6	7	8
12	13	14	15
19	20	21	22
26	27	28	29

"I don't know what the future may hold,
but I know who holds the future."
-- Ralph Abernathy

Thursday	Friday	Saturday	NOTES
2	3	4	
9	10	11	
16	17	18	
23	24	25	
30	31		

Independence Day (in the Saturday 4 cell)

August 2026

Sunday	Monday	Tuesday	Wednesday
2	3	4	5
9	10	11	12
16	17	18	19
23 30	24 31	25	26

"You have to learn the rules to be able to know how to break them."
-- Keira Knightley

Thursday	Friday	Saturday	NOTES
		1	
6	7	8	
13	14	15	
20	21	22	
27	28	29	

September 2026

Sunday	Monday	Tuesday	Wednesday
		1	2
6	7	8	9
	Labor Day		
13	14	15	16
20	21	22	23
27	28	29	30

"It's a gift to exist, and with existence comes suffering.
There's no escaping that."
-- Stephen Colbert

Thursday	Friday	Saturday	NOTES
3	4	5	
10	11	12	
17	18	19	
24	25	26	

October 2026

Sunday	Monday	Tuesday	Wednesday
4	5	6	7
11	12 *Columbus Day*	13	14
18	19	20	21
25	26	27	28

"All good ideas start out as bad ideas, that's why it takes so long."
-- Steven Spielberg

Thursday	Friday	Saturday	NOTES
1	2	3	
8	9	10	
15	16	17	
22	23	24	
29	30	31 *Halloween*	

November 2026

Sunday	Monday	Tuesday	Wednesday
1	2	3	4
8	9	10	11 *Vaterans Day*
15	16	17	18
22	23	24	25
29	30		

"People who think they know everything
are a great annoyance to those of us who do."
-- Isaac Asimov

Thursday	Friday	Saturday	NOTES
5	6	7	
12	13	14	
19	20	21	
26 *Thanksgiving Day*	27 *Black Friday*	28	

December 2026

Sunday	Monday	Tuesday	Wednesday
		1	2
6	7	8	9
13	14	15	16
20	21	22	23
27	28	29	30

"Fail fast. Fail often... The most talented people in the world have bad ideas.
That's a good thing to learn."
-- Rashida Jones

Thursday	Friday	Saturday	NOTES
3	4	5	
10	11	12	
17	18	19	
24	25	26	
Christmas Eve	Christmas Day		
31			
New Year's Eve			

Notes

Many Thanks